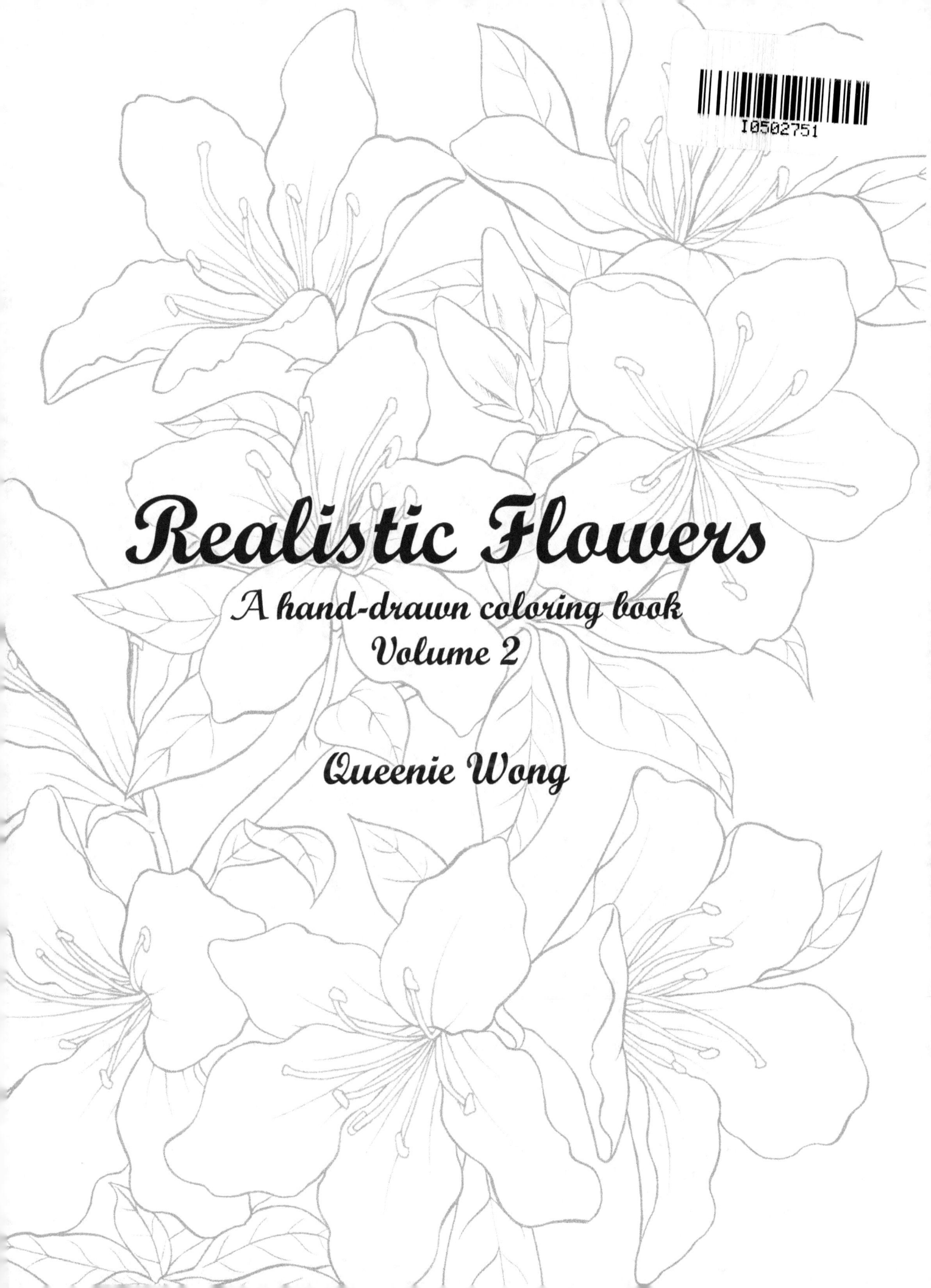

Realistic Flowers
A hand-drawn coloring book
Volume 2

Queenie Wong

ISBN-13: 978-1542393195
ISBN-10: 1542393191
First published in United States in 2017
Illustrations by Queenie Wong
Wonger0050@yahoo.com.hk

List of 25 kinds of flowers in this book:

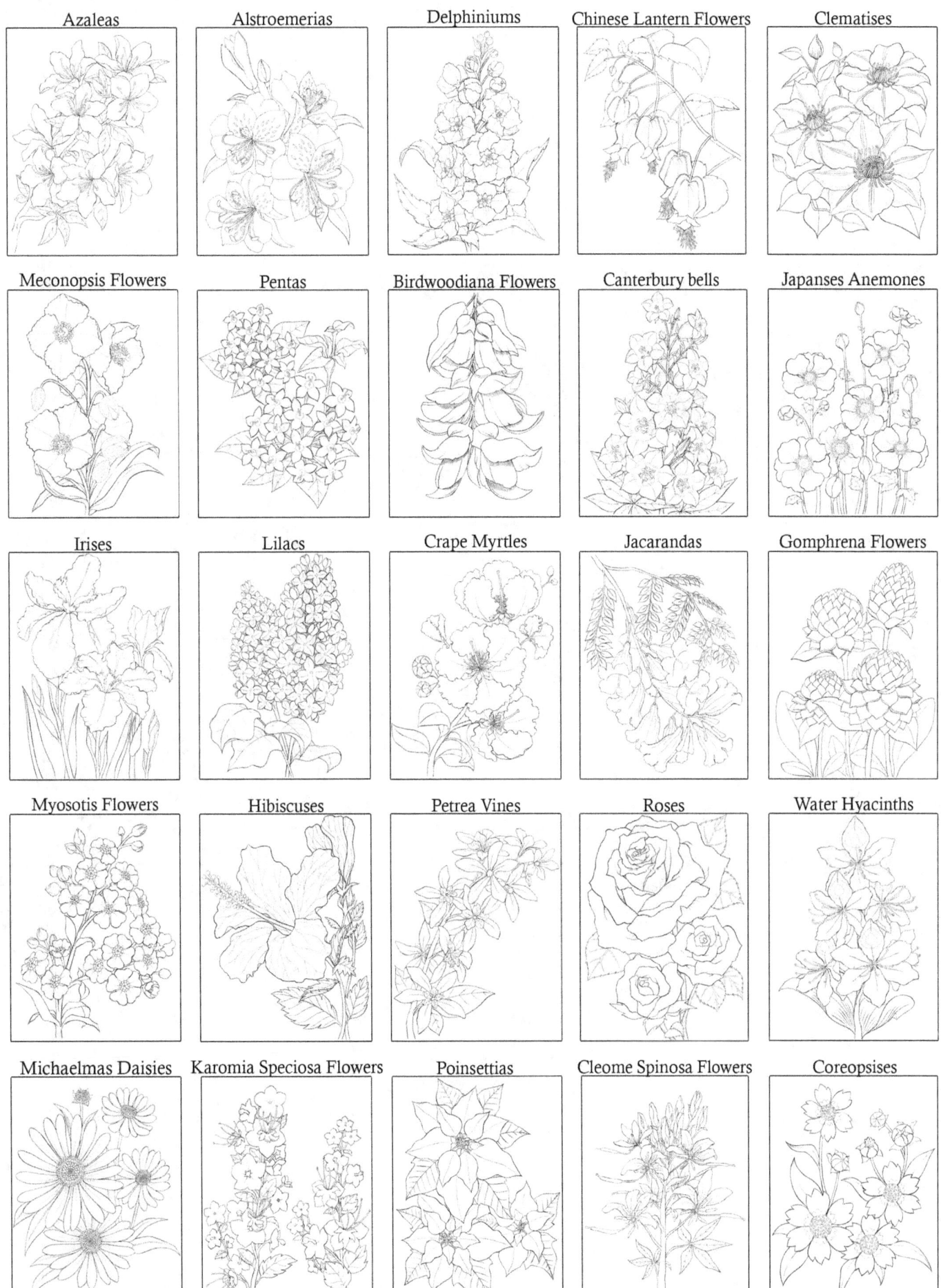

Azaleas	Alstroemerias	Delphiniums	Chinese Lantern Flowers	Clematises
Meconopsis Flowers	Pentas	Birdwoodiana Flowers	Canterbury bells	Japanses Anemones
Irises	Lilacs	Crape Myrtles	Jacarandas	Gomphrena Flowers
Myosotis Flowers	Hibiscuses	Petrea Vines	Roses	Water Hyacinths
Michaelmas Daisies	Karomia Speciosa Flowers	Poinsettias	Cleome Spinosa Flowers	Coreopsises

Azaleas

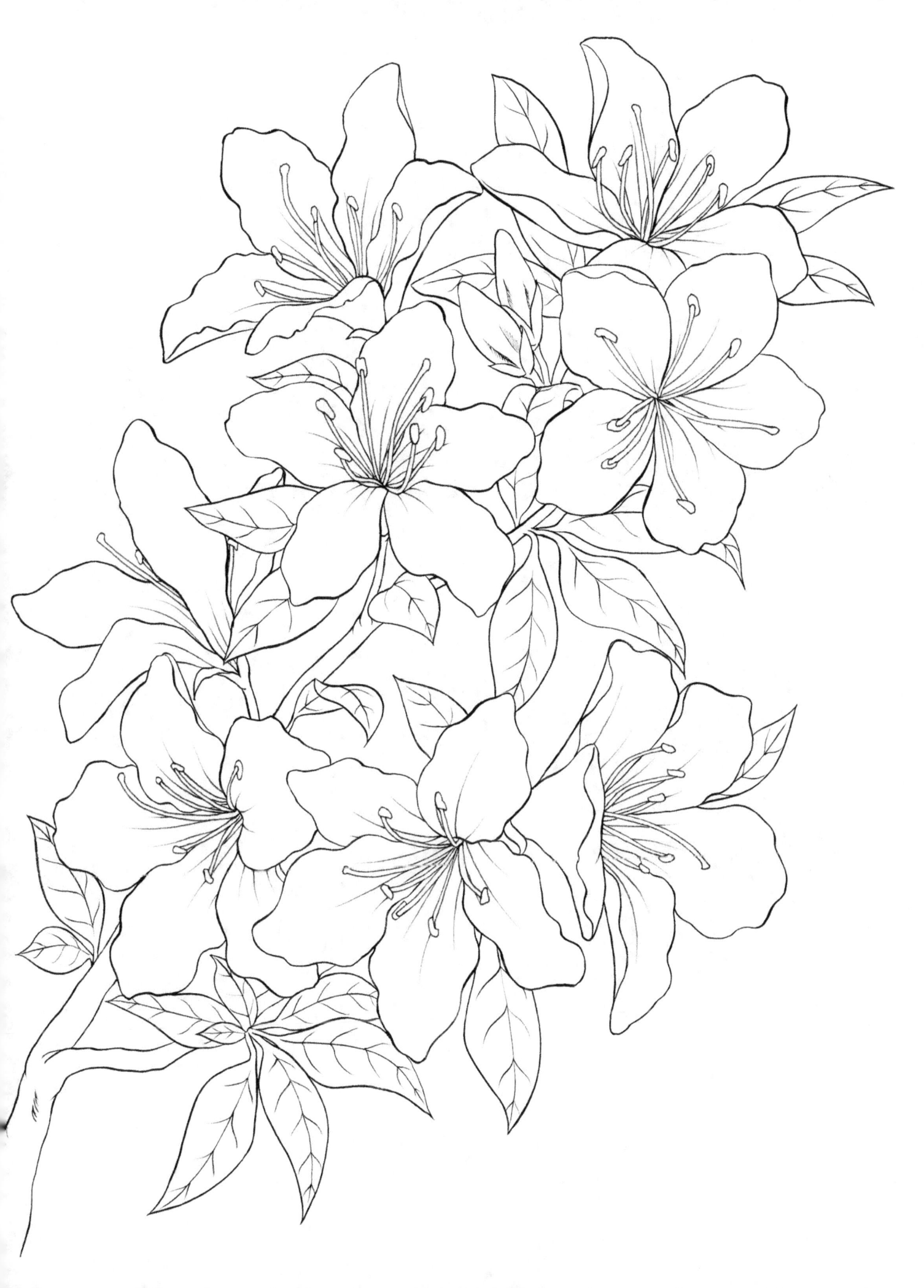

Alstroemerias

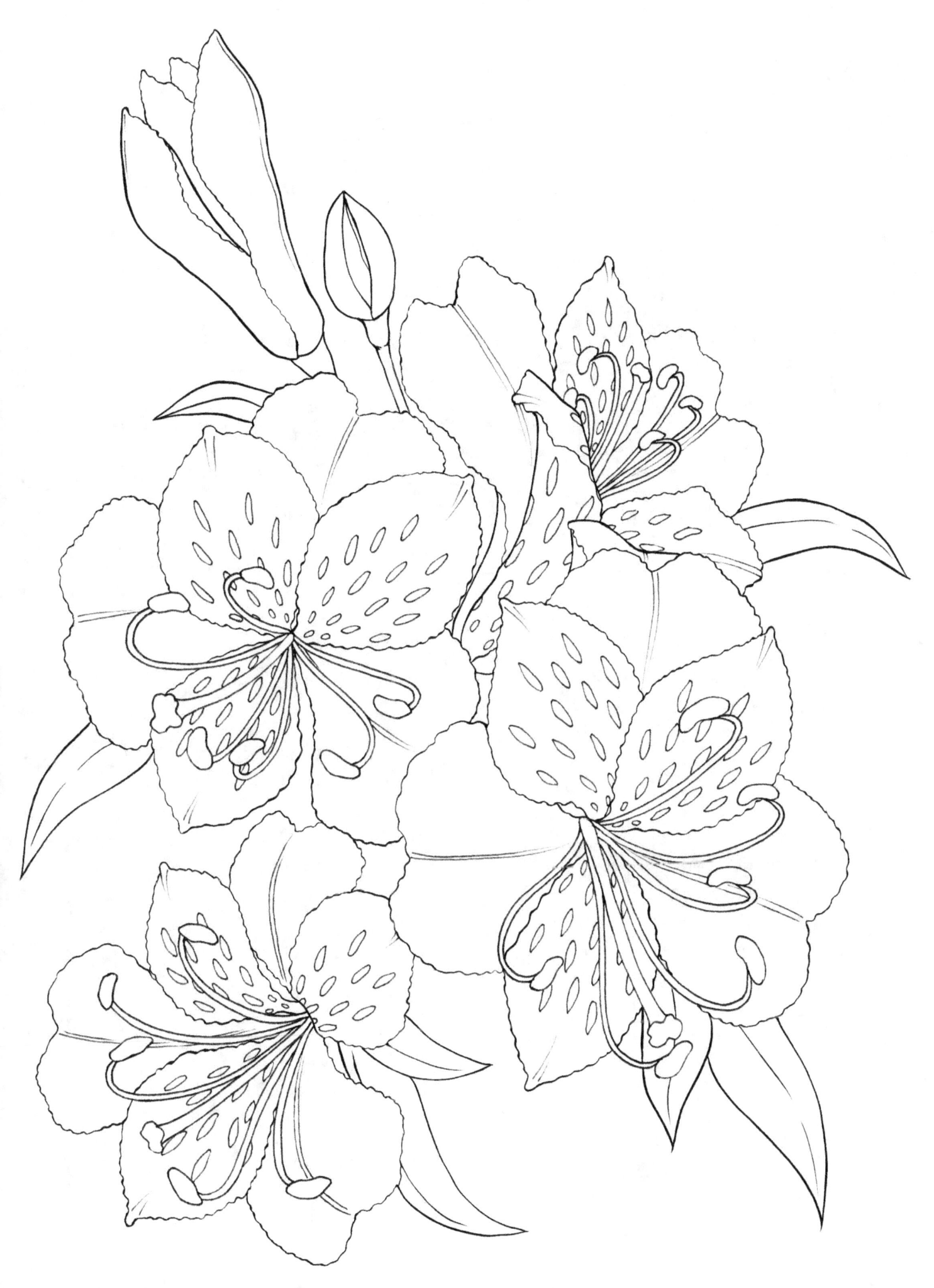

Delphiniums

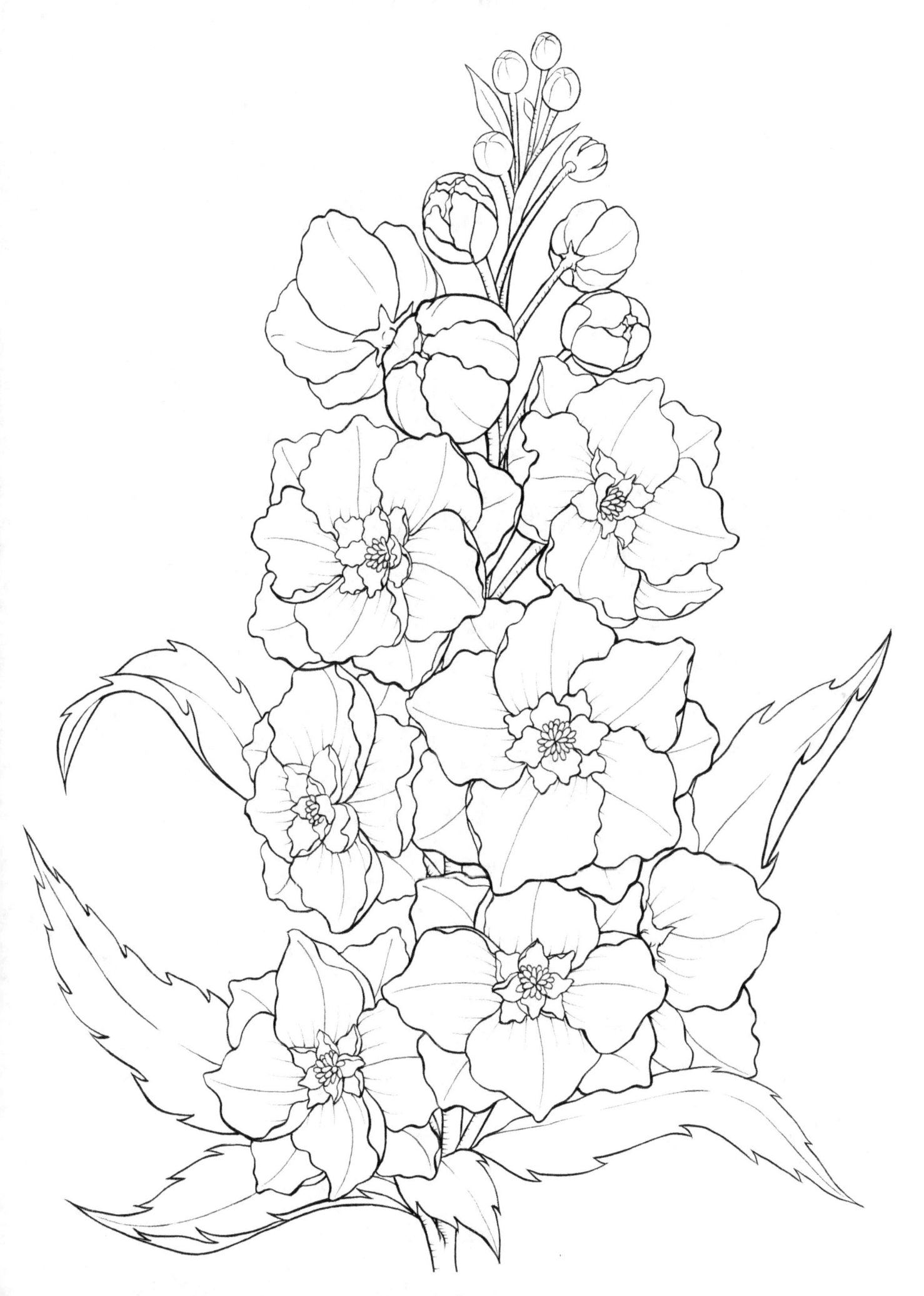

Chinese Lantern Flowers

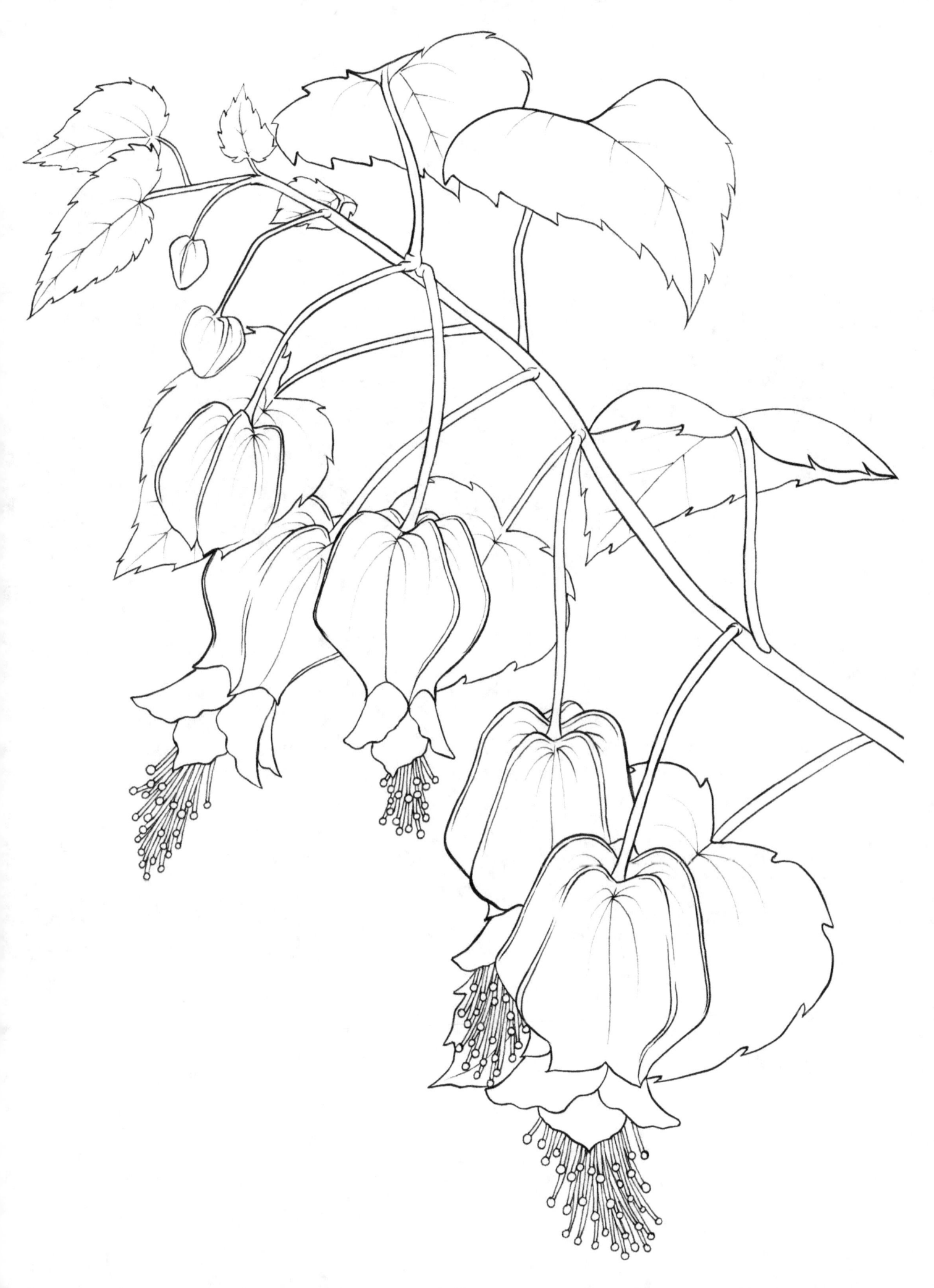

Clematises

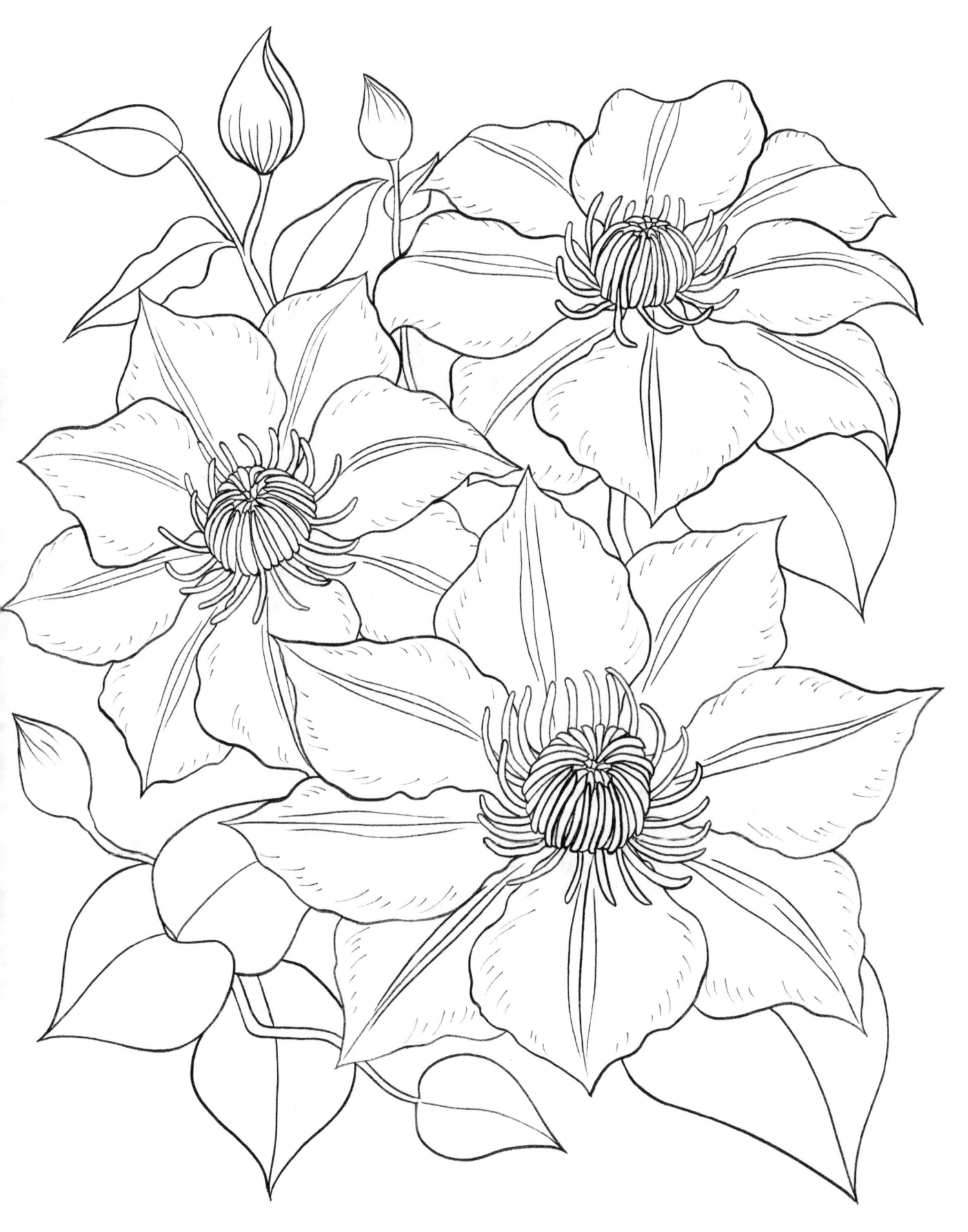

Meconopsis Flowers

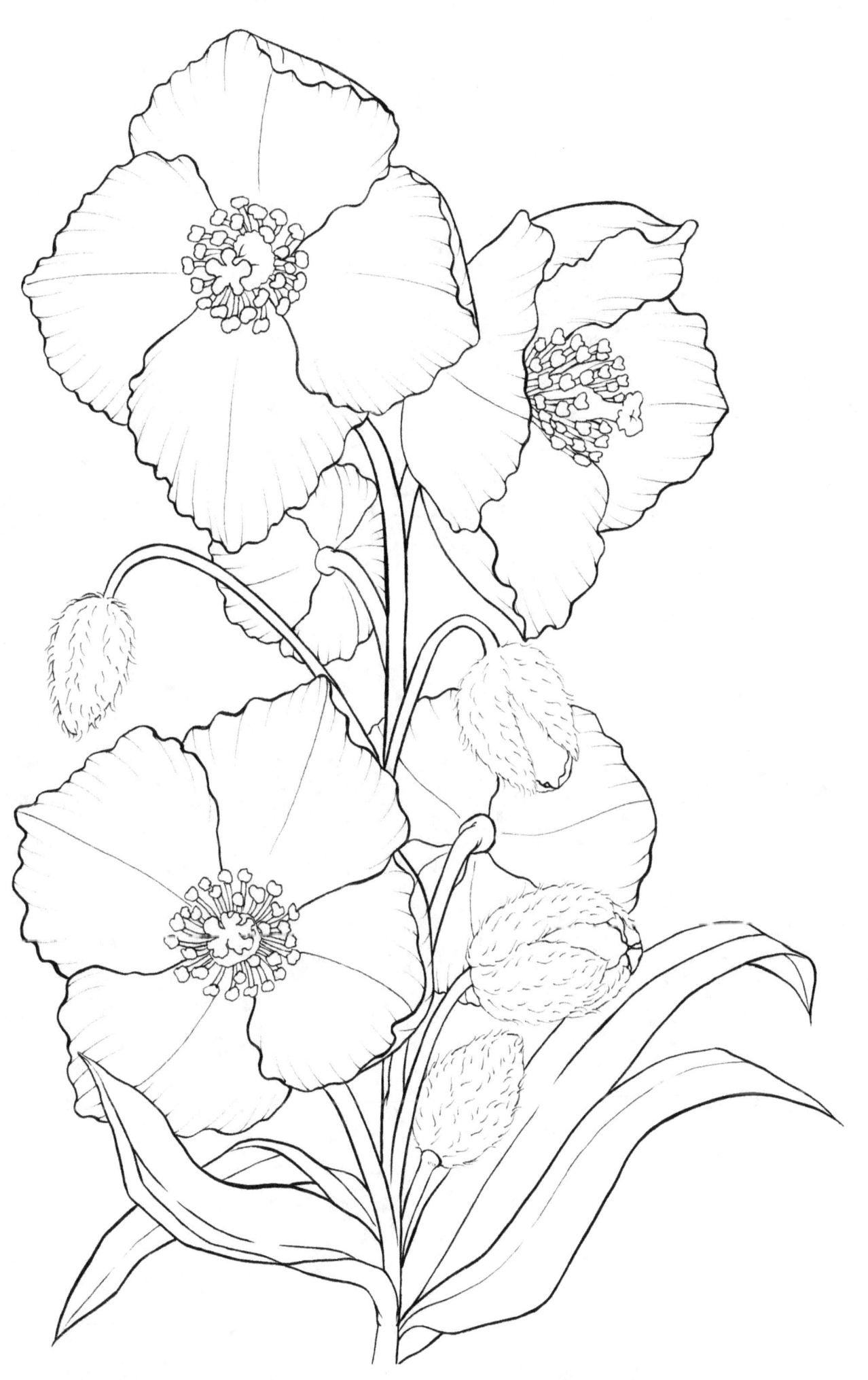

Pentas

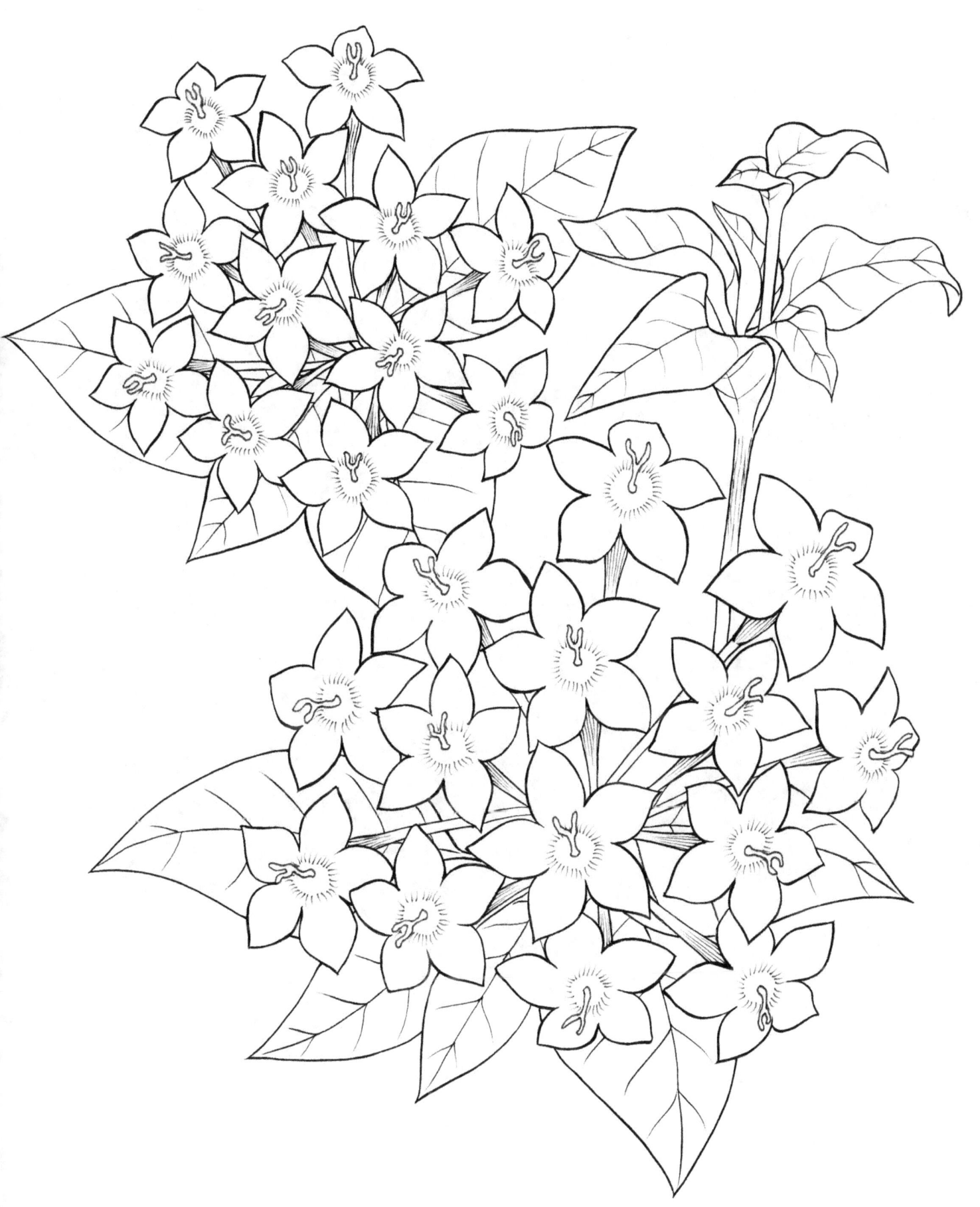

Birdwoodiana Flowers

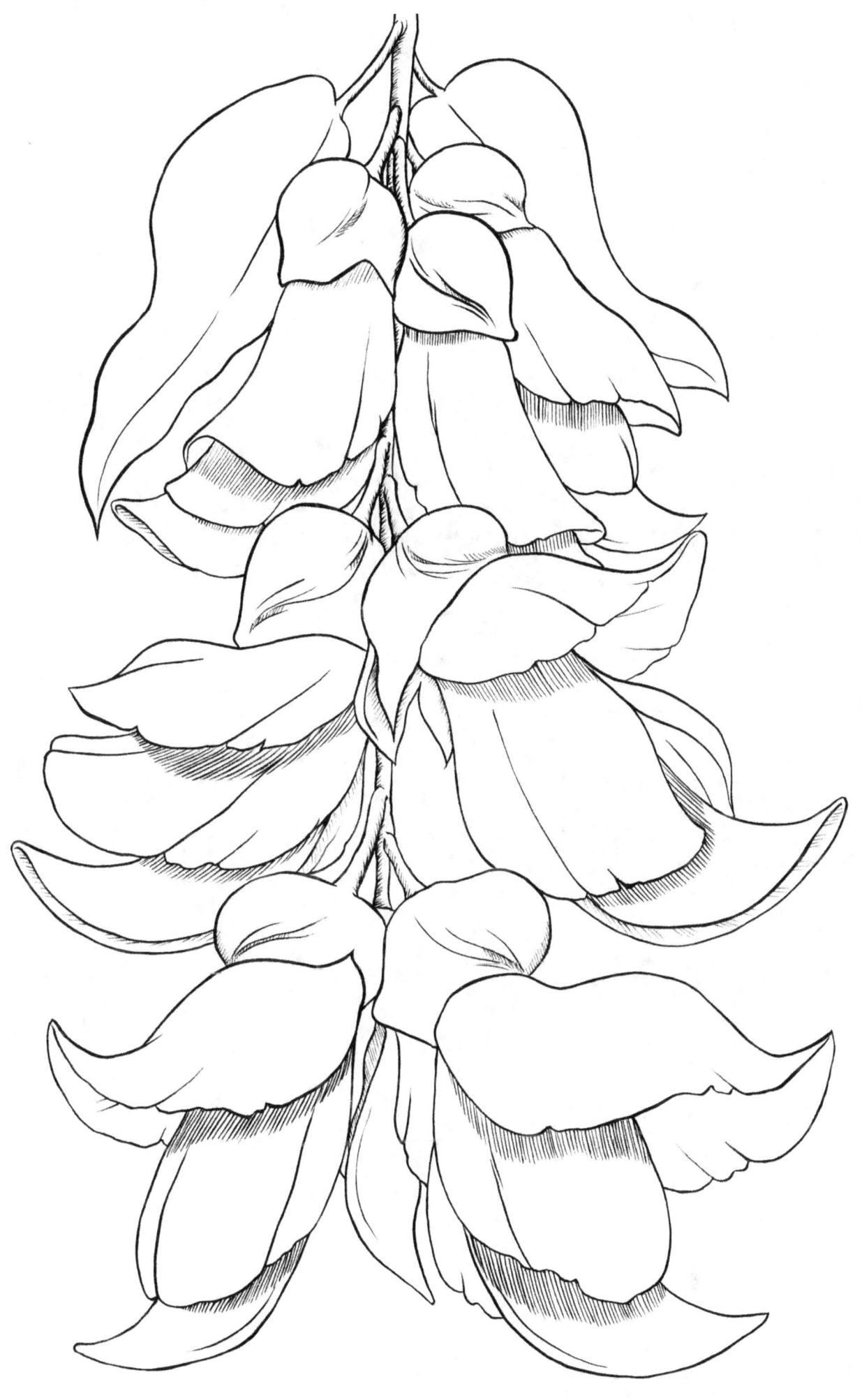

Canterbury Bells

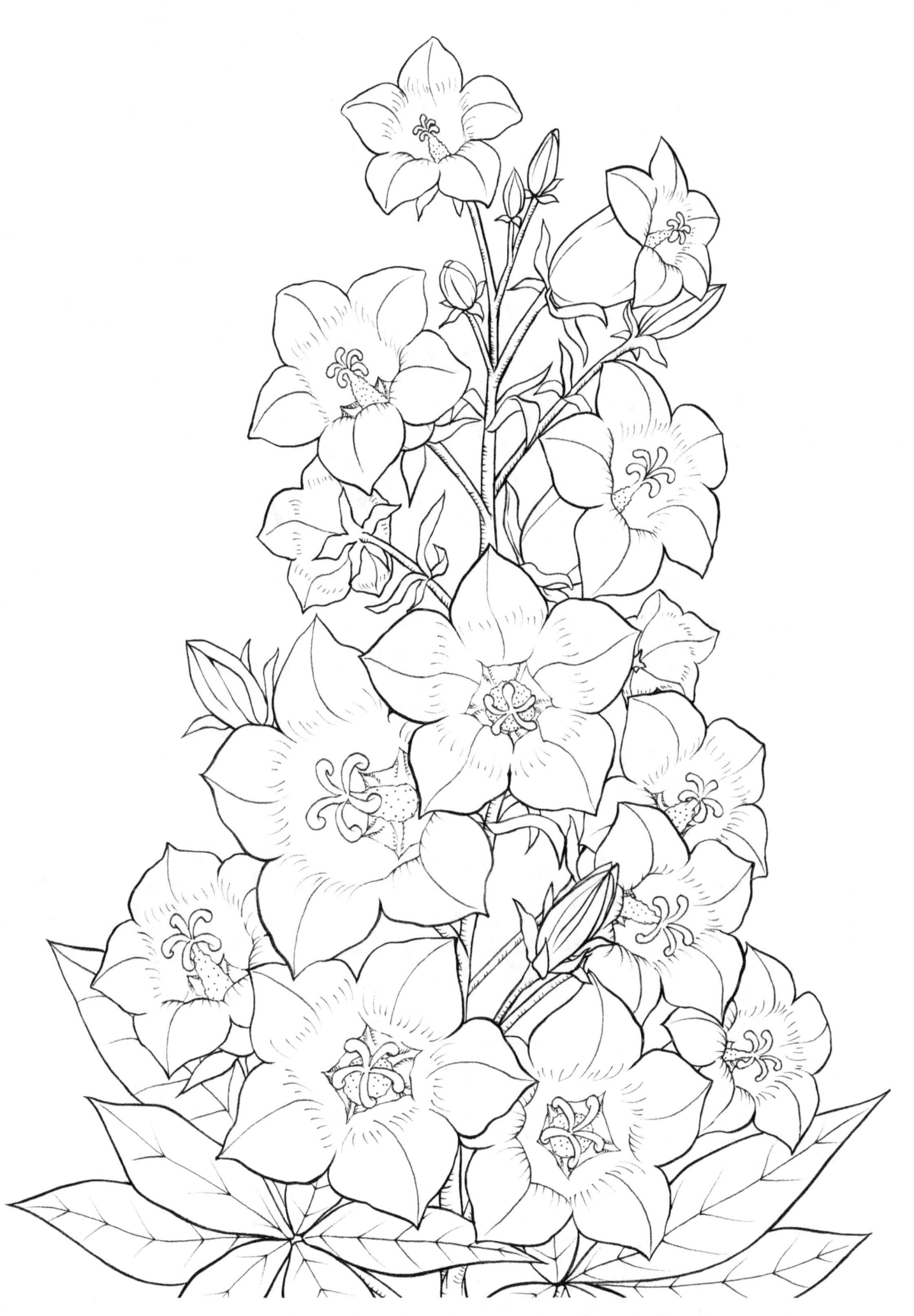

Japanese Anemones

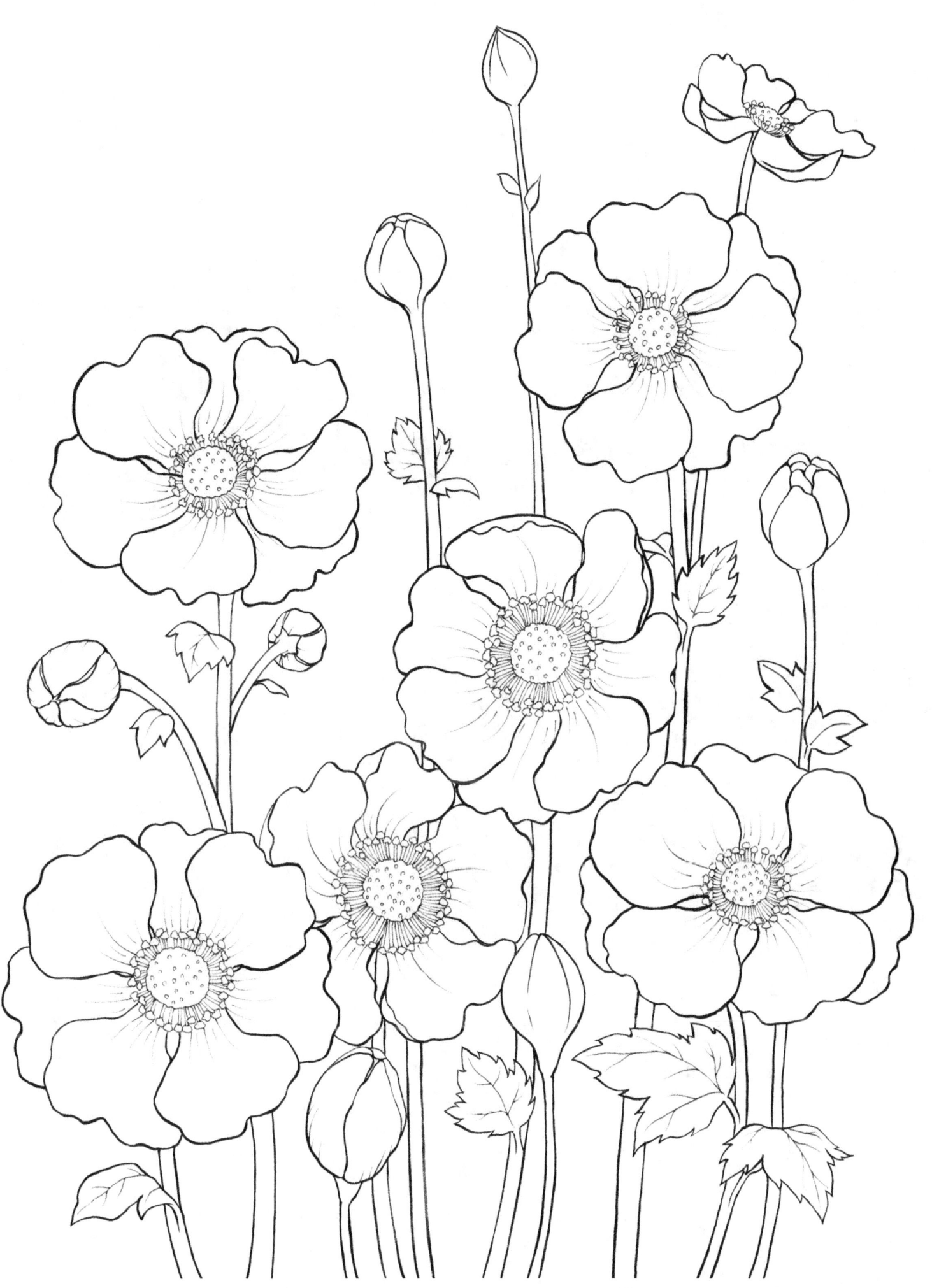

Irises

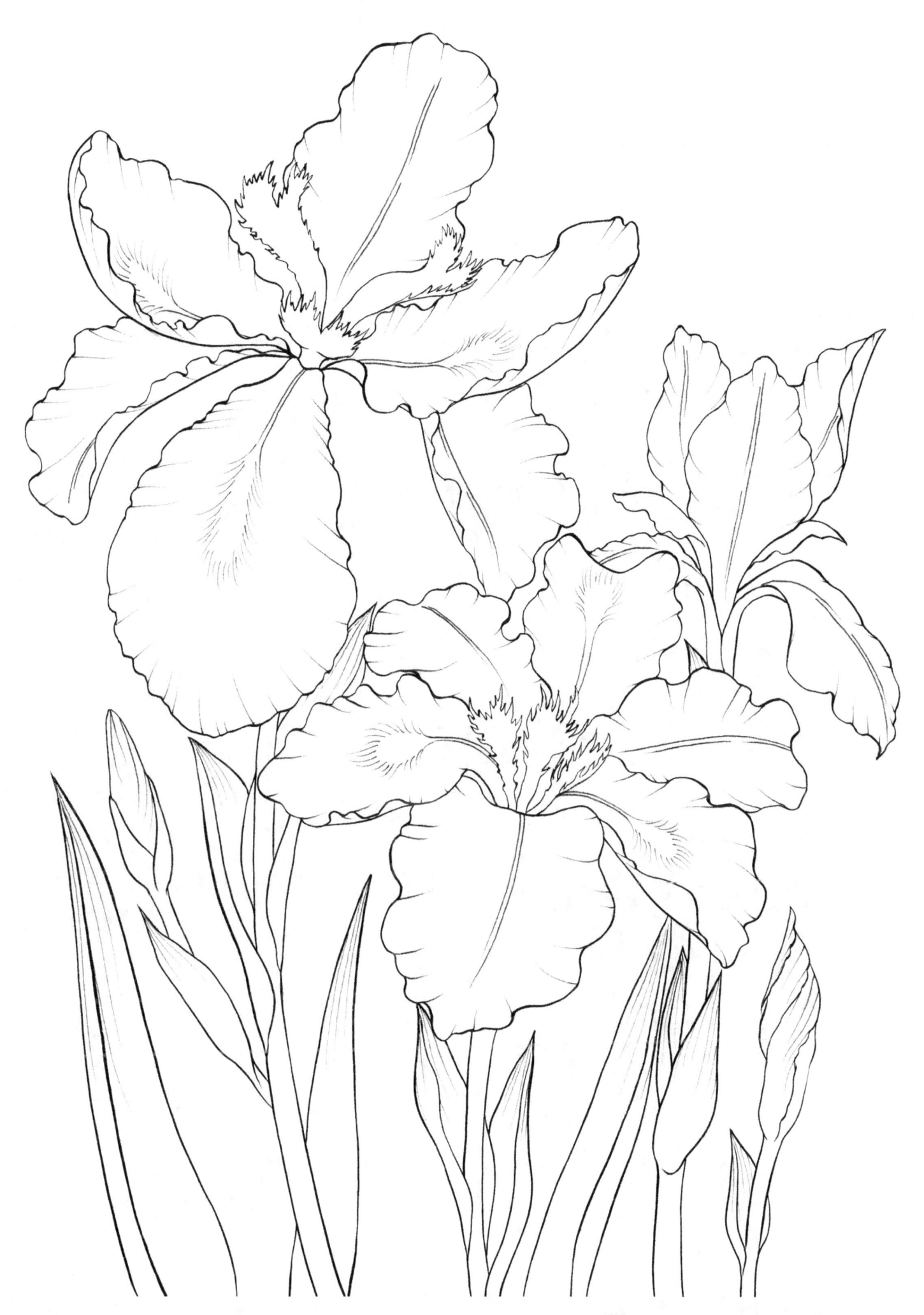

Lilacs

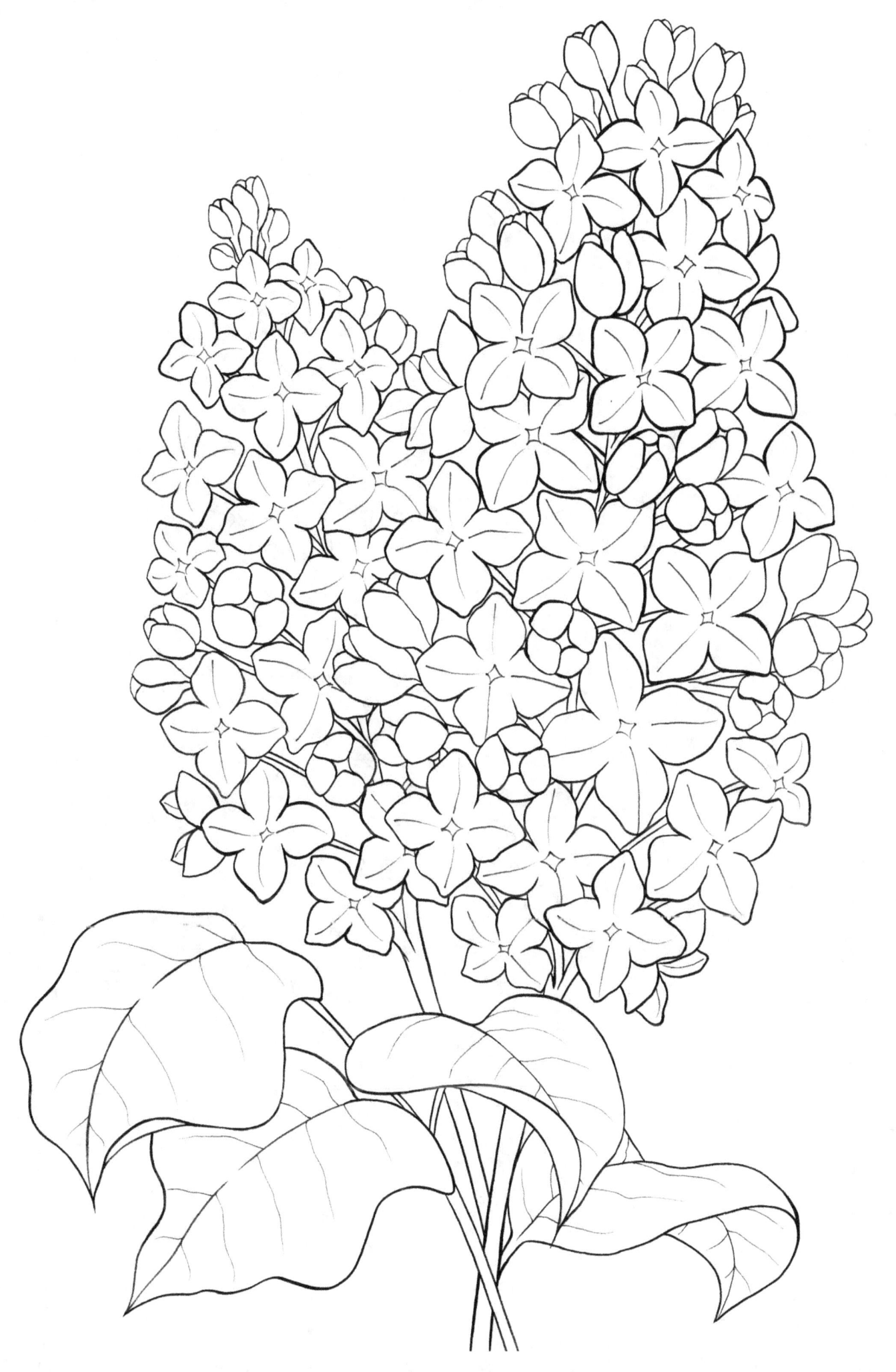

Crape Myrtles

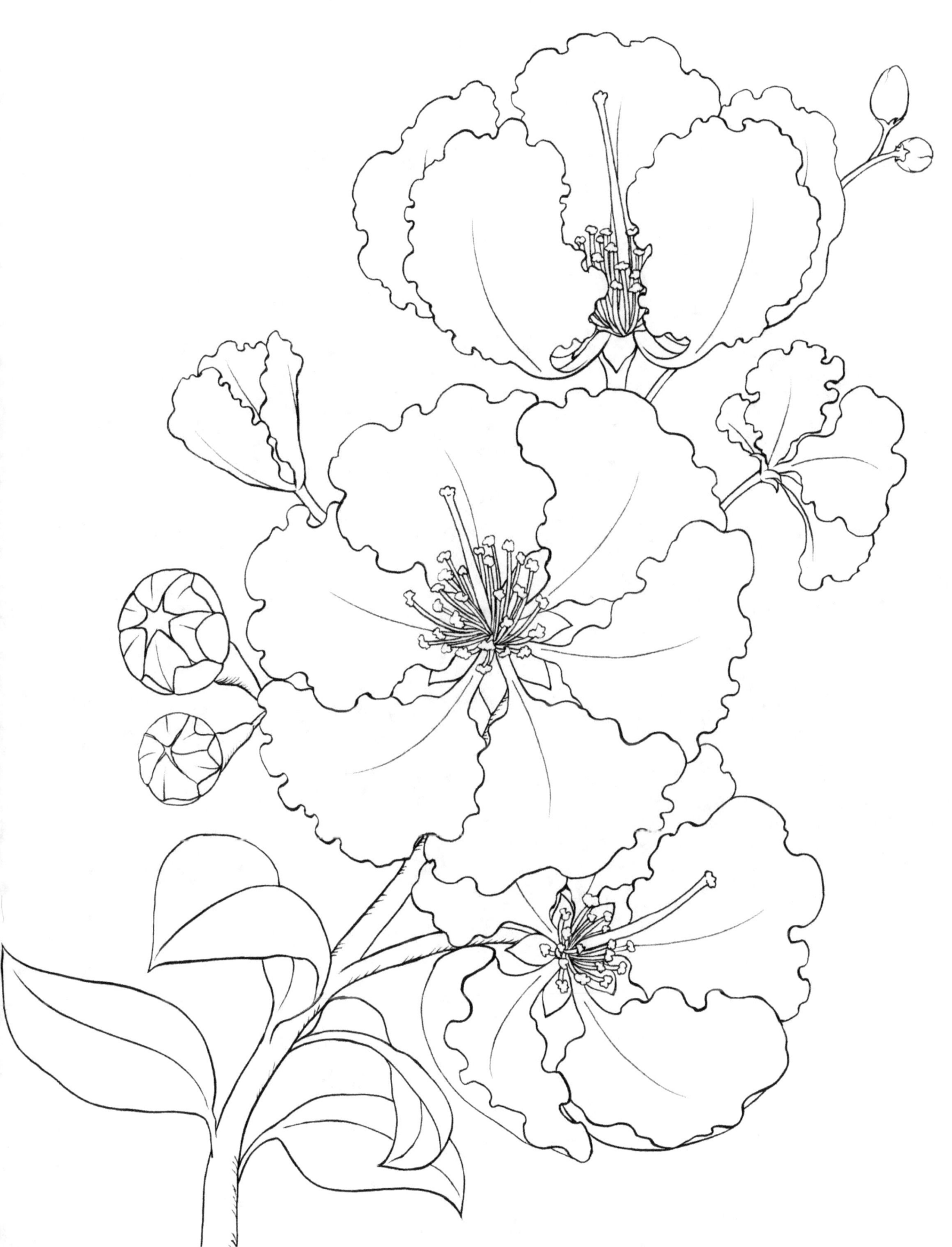

Jacarandas

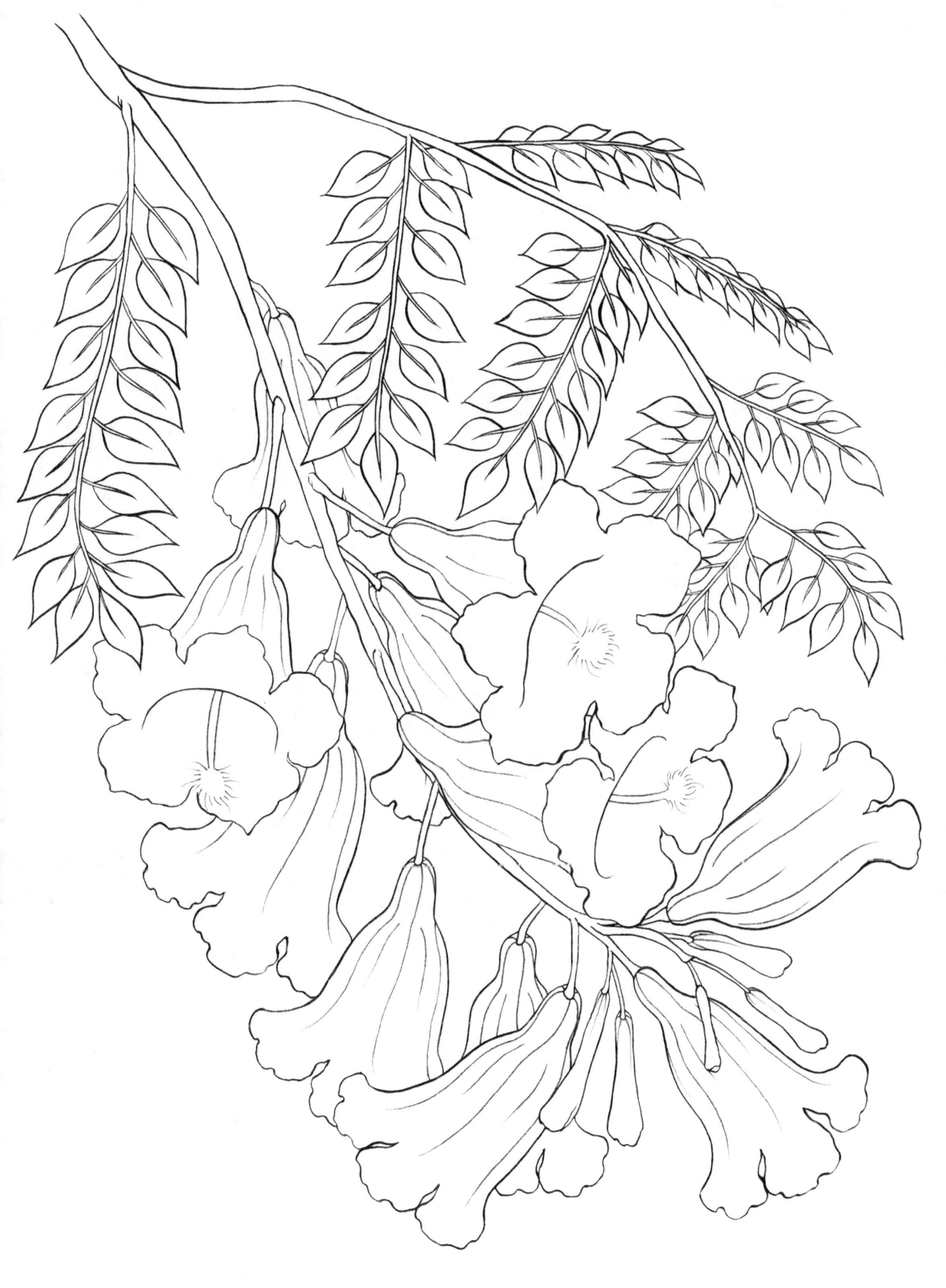

Gomphrena Flowers

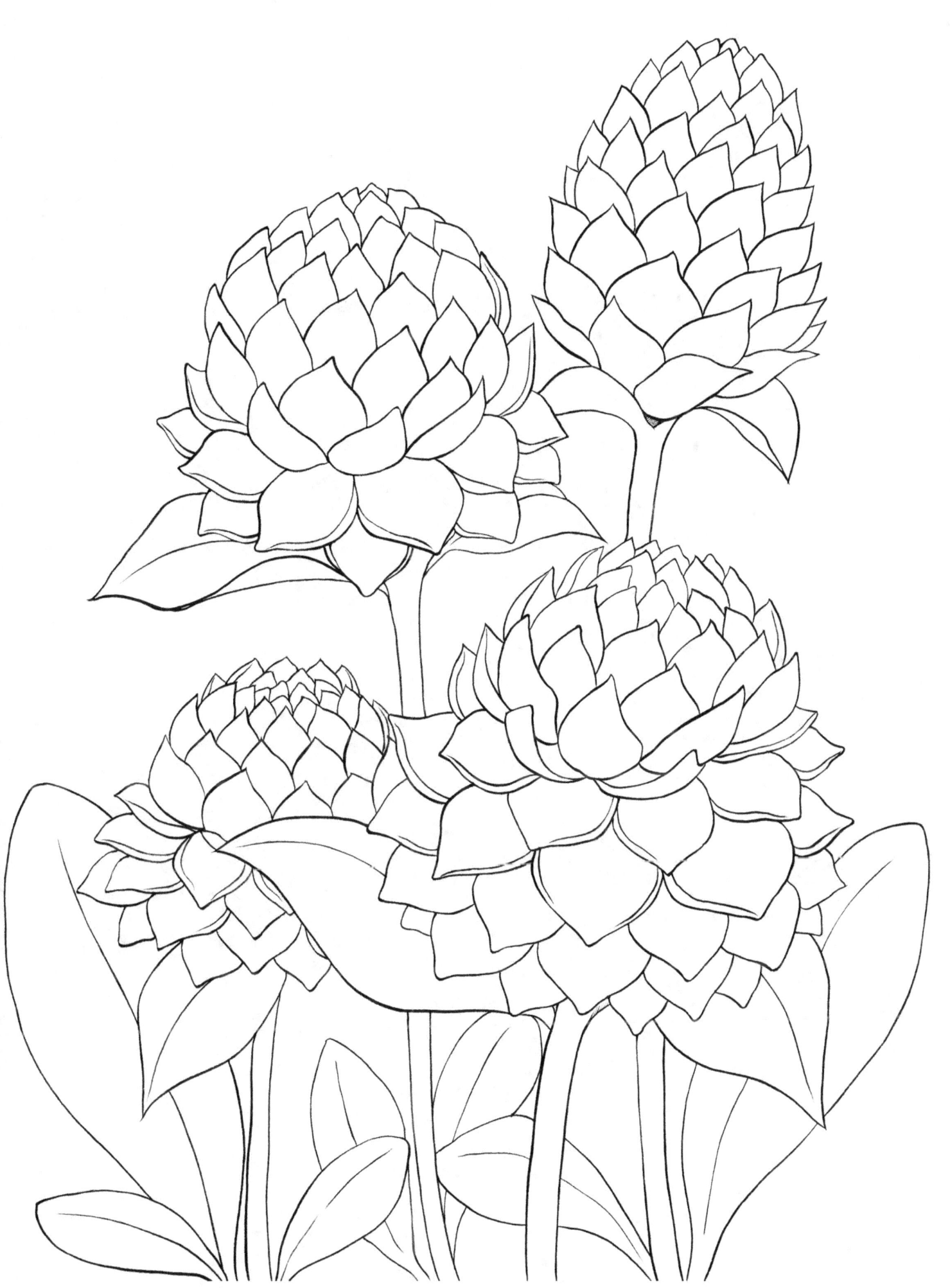

Myosotis Flowers

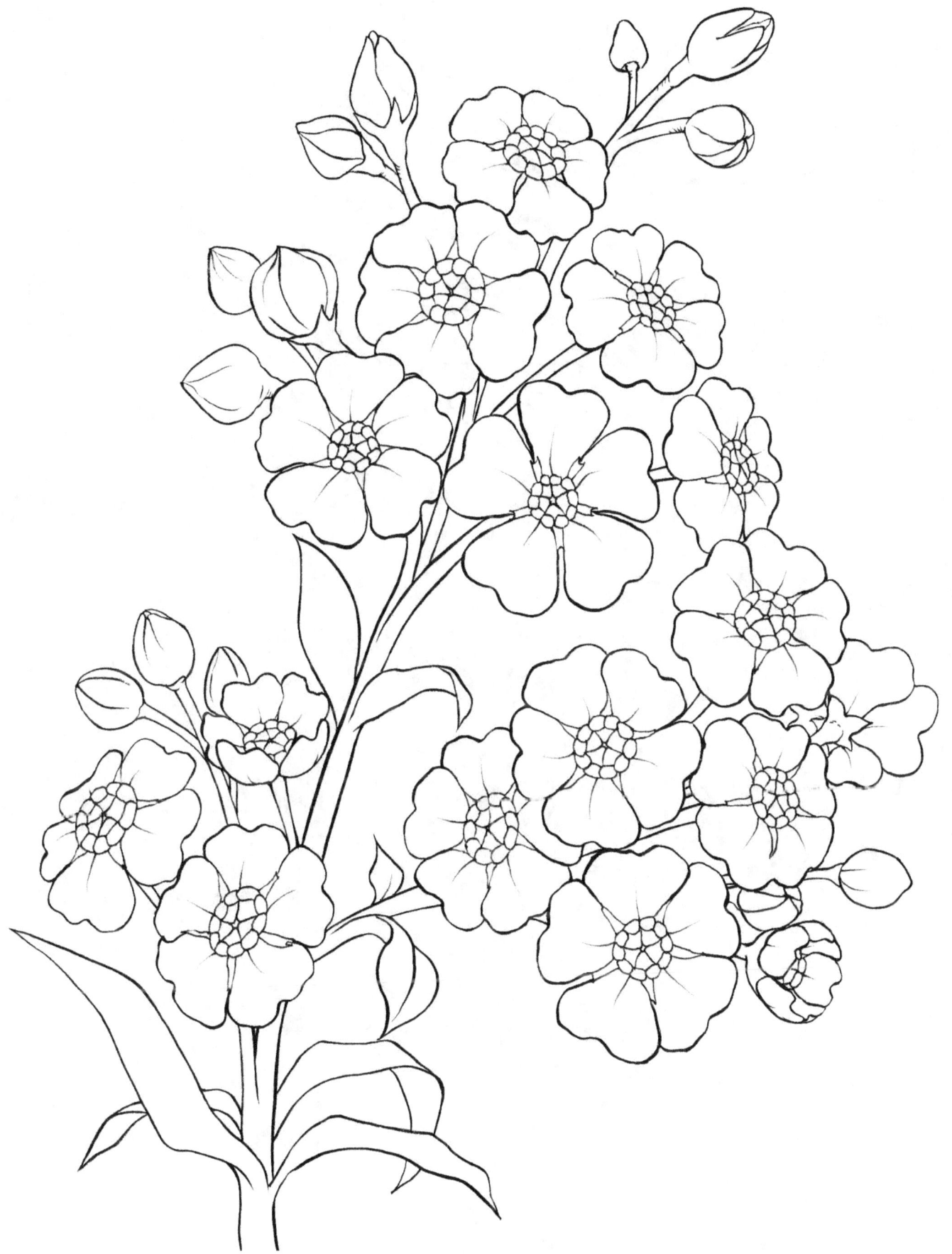

Hibiscuses

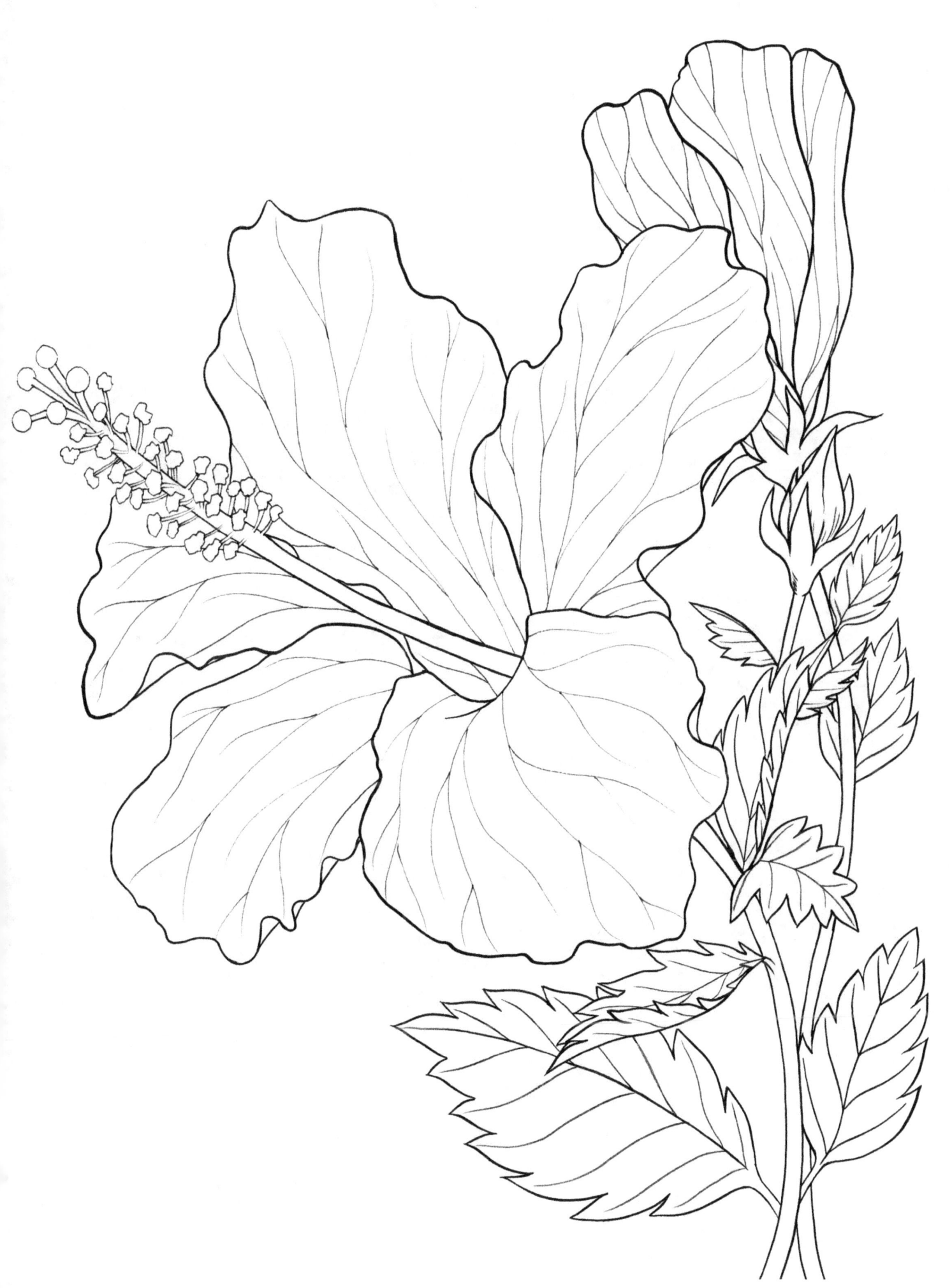

Petrea Vines

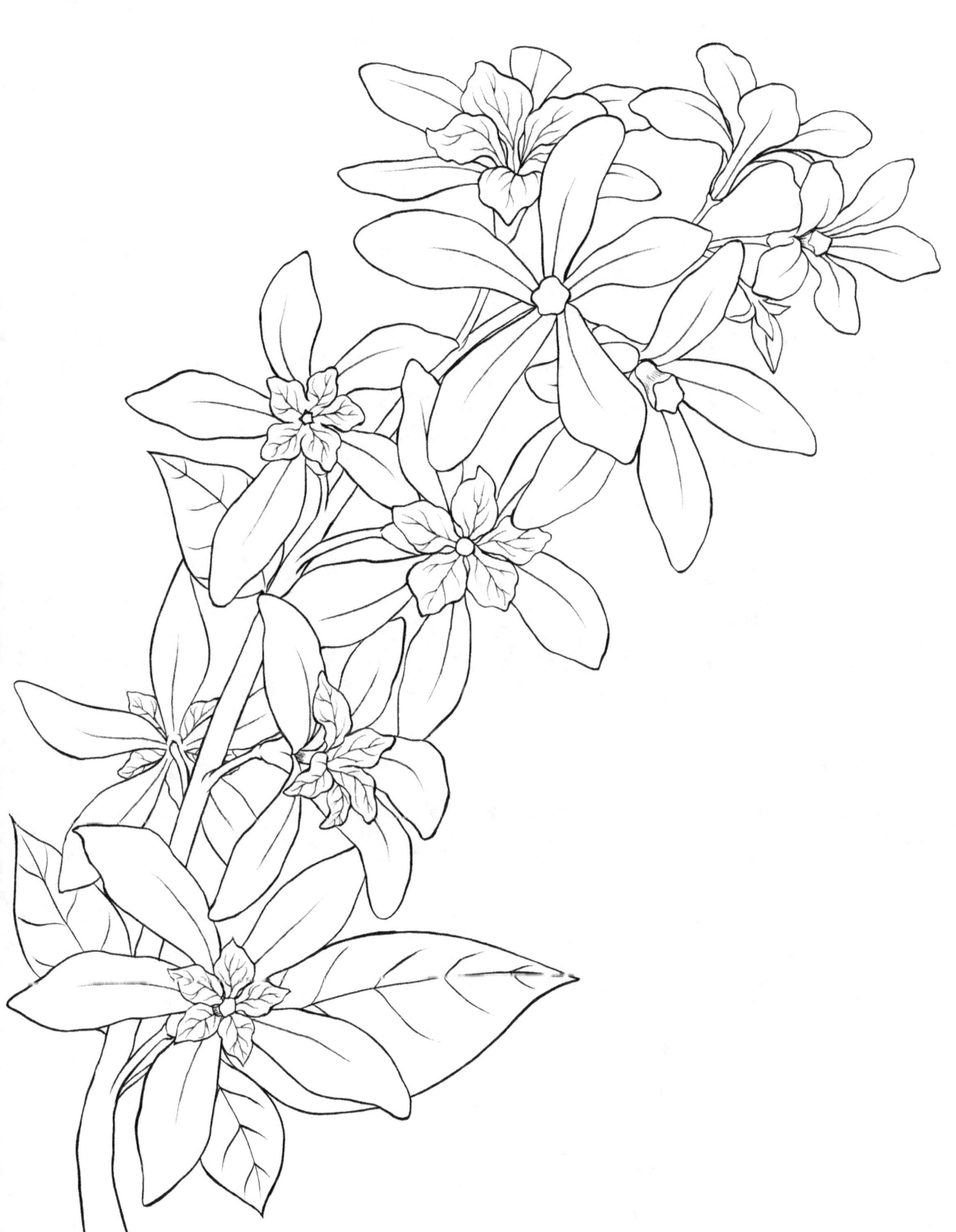

Roses

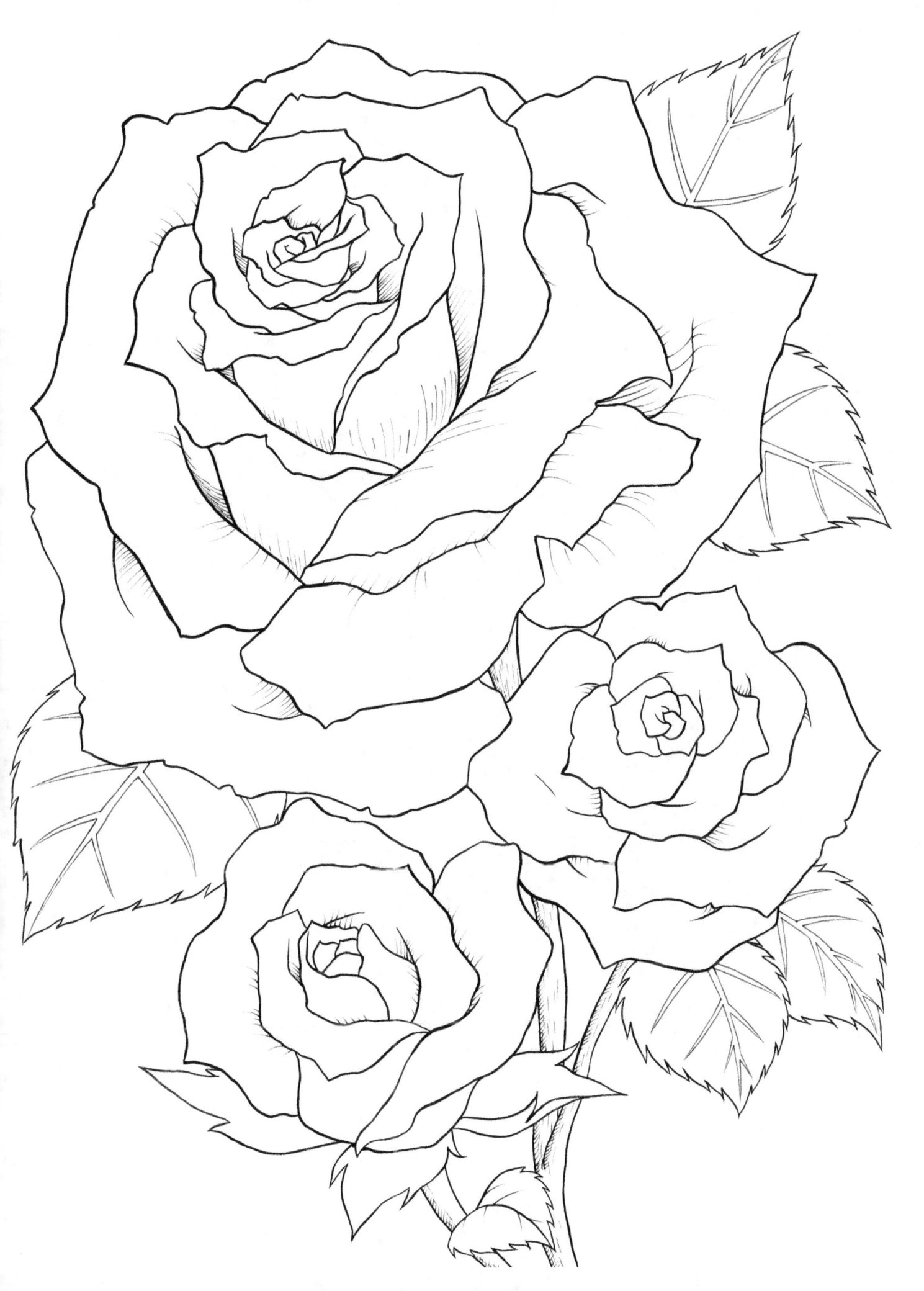

Water Hyacinths

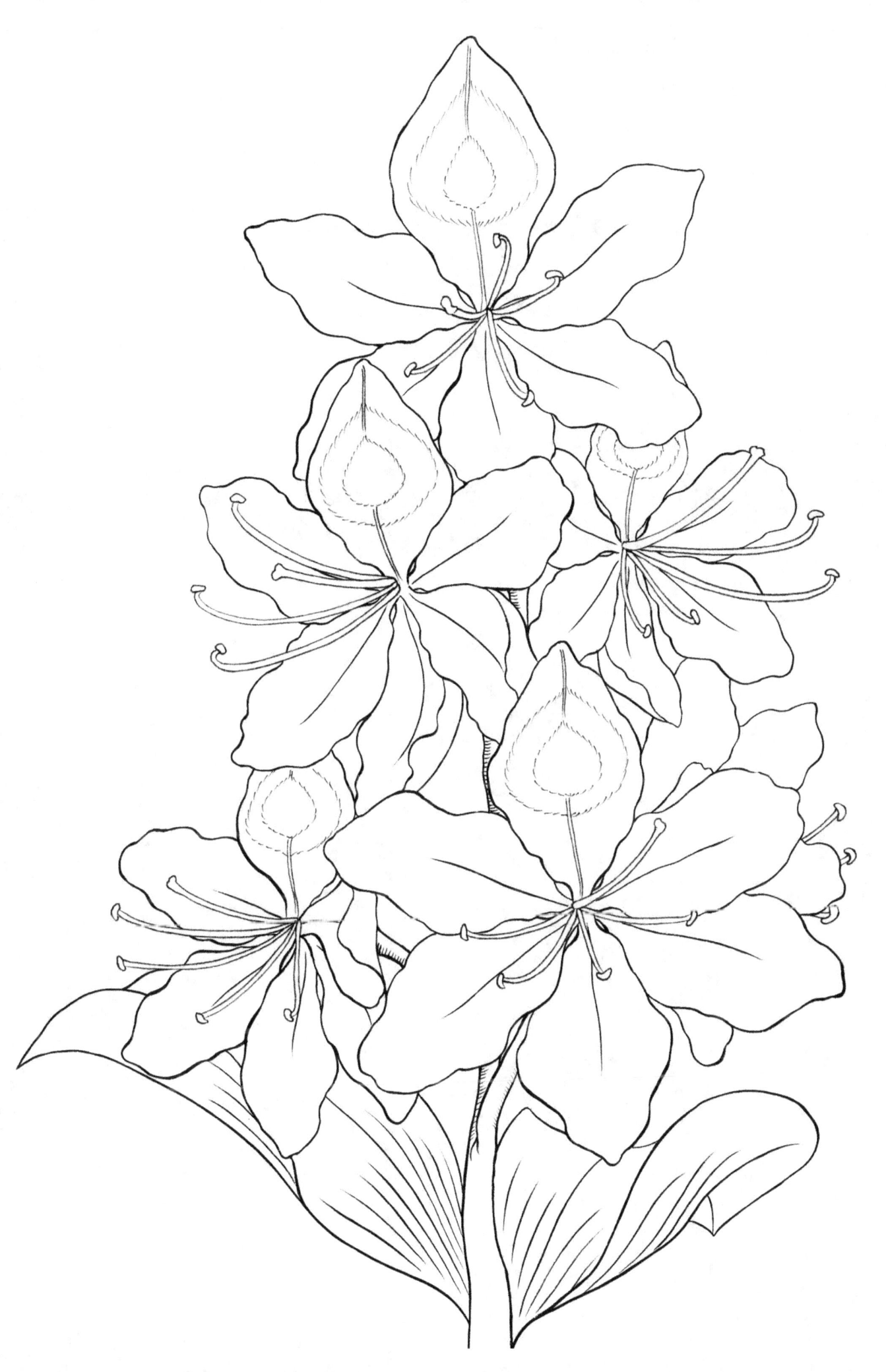

Michaelmas Daisies

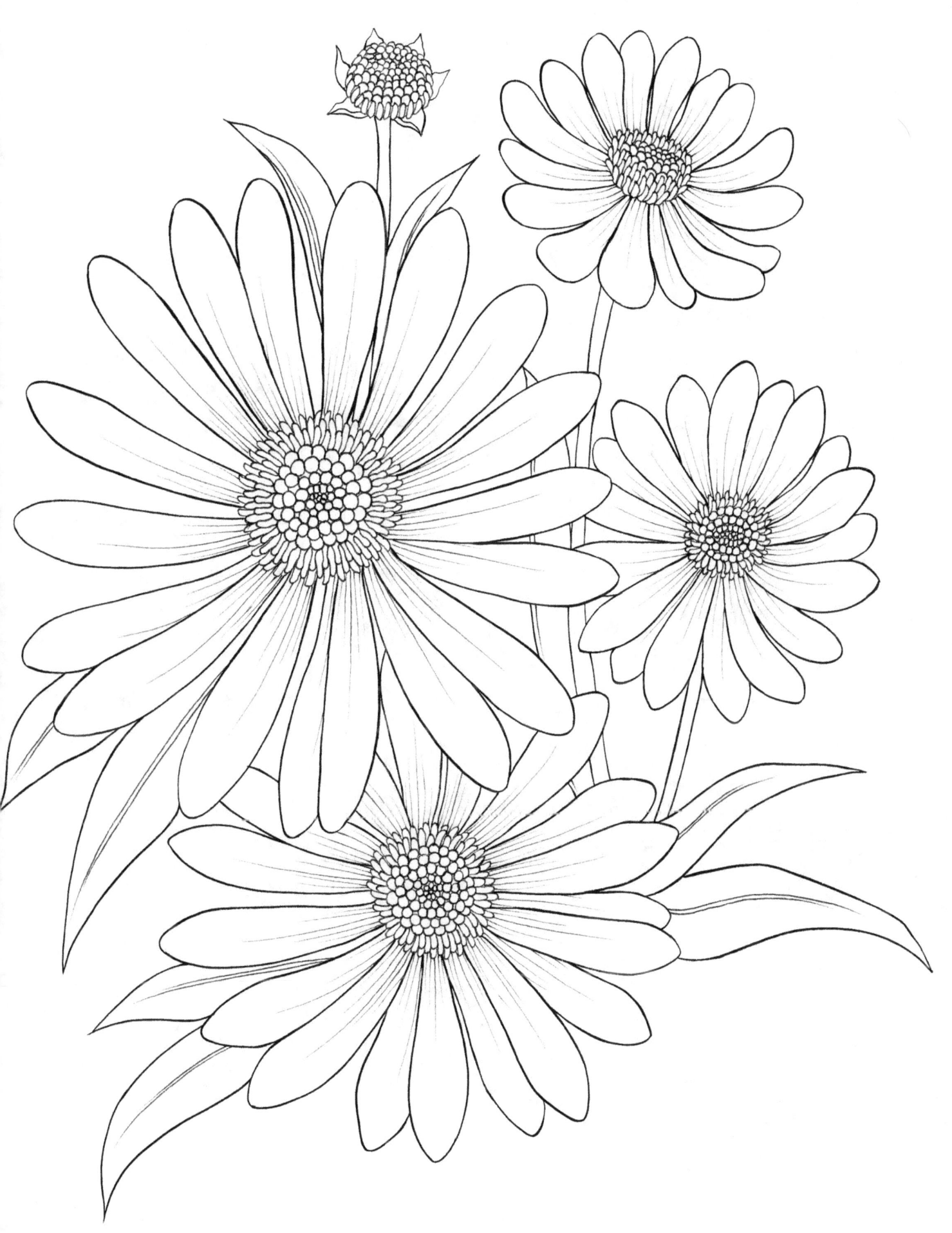

Karomia Speciosa Flowers

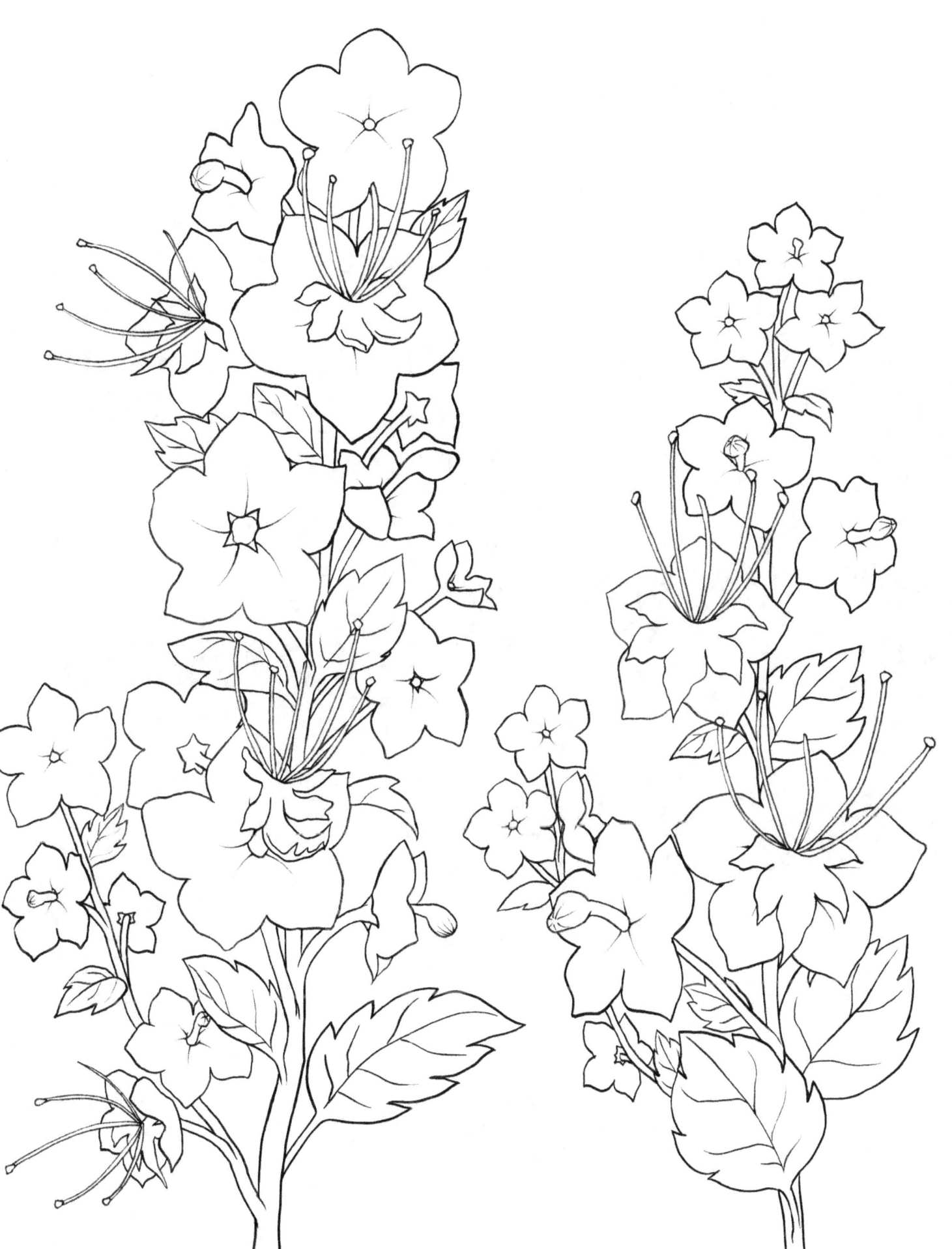

Poinsettias

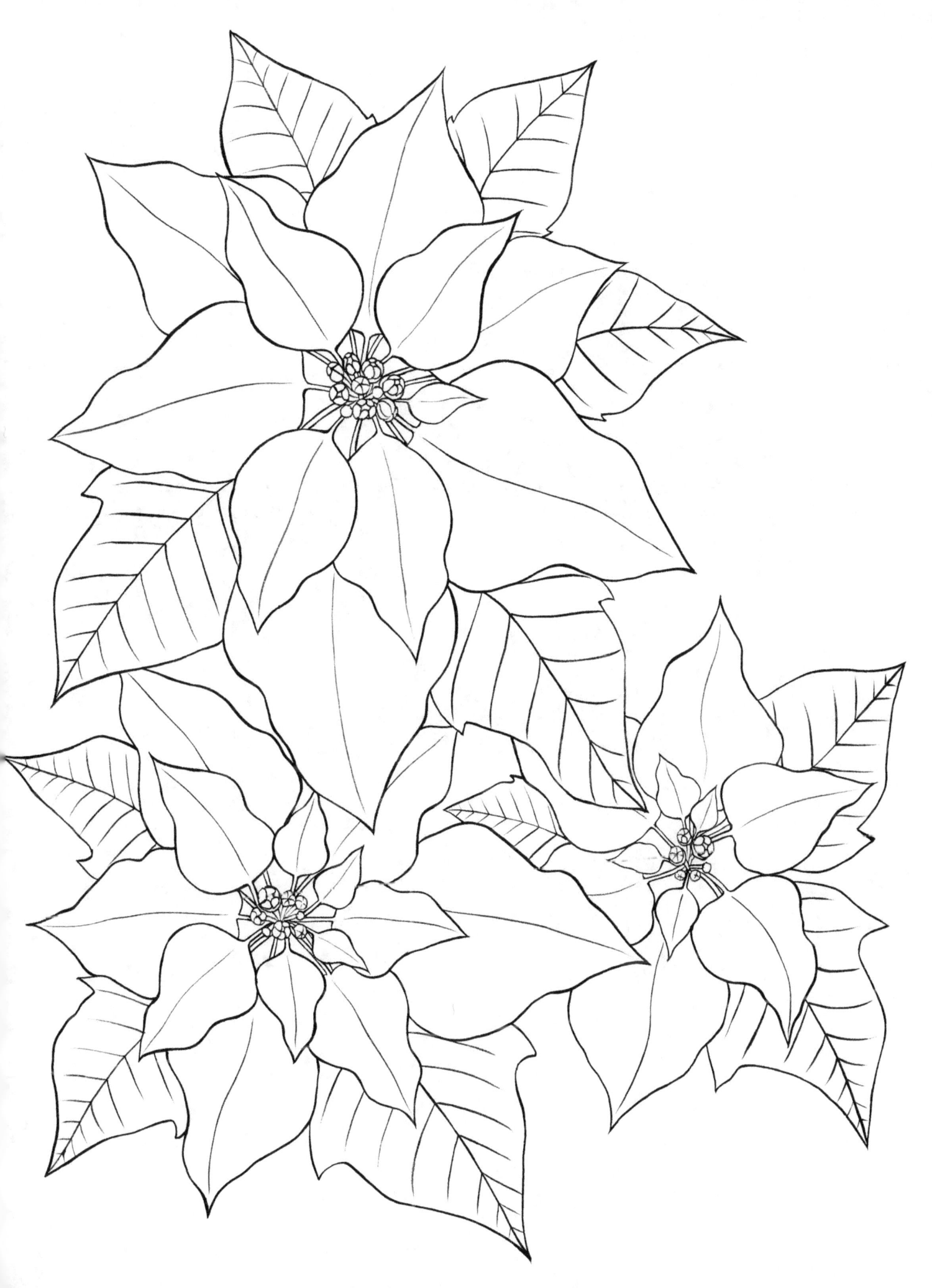

Cleome Spinosa Flowers

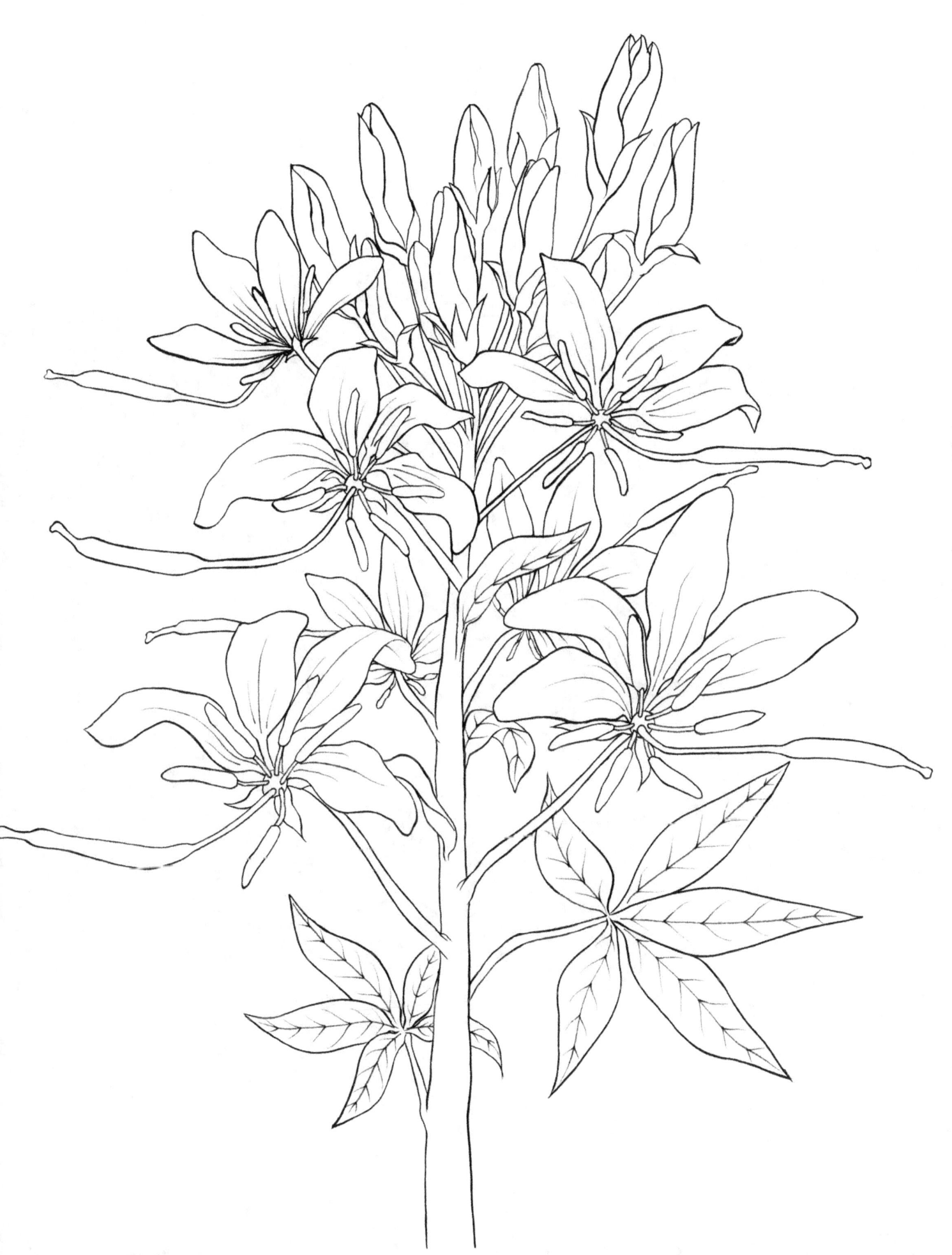

Coreopsises

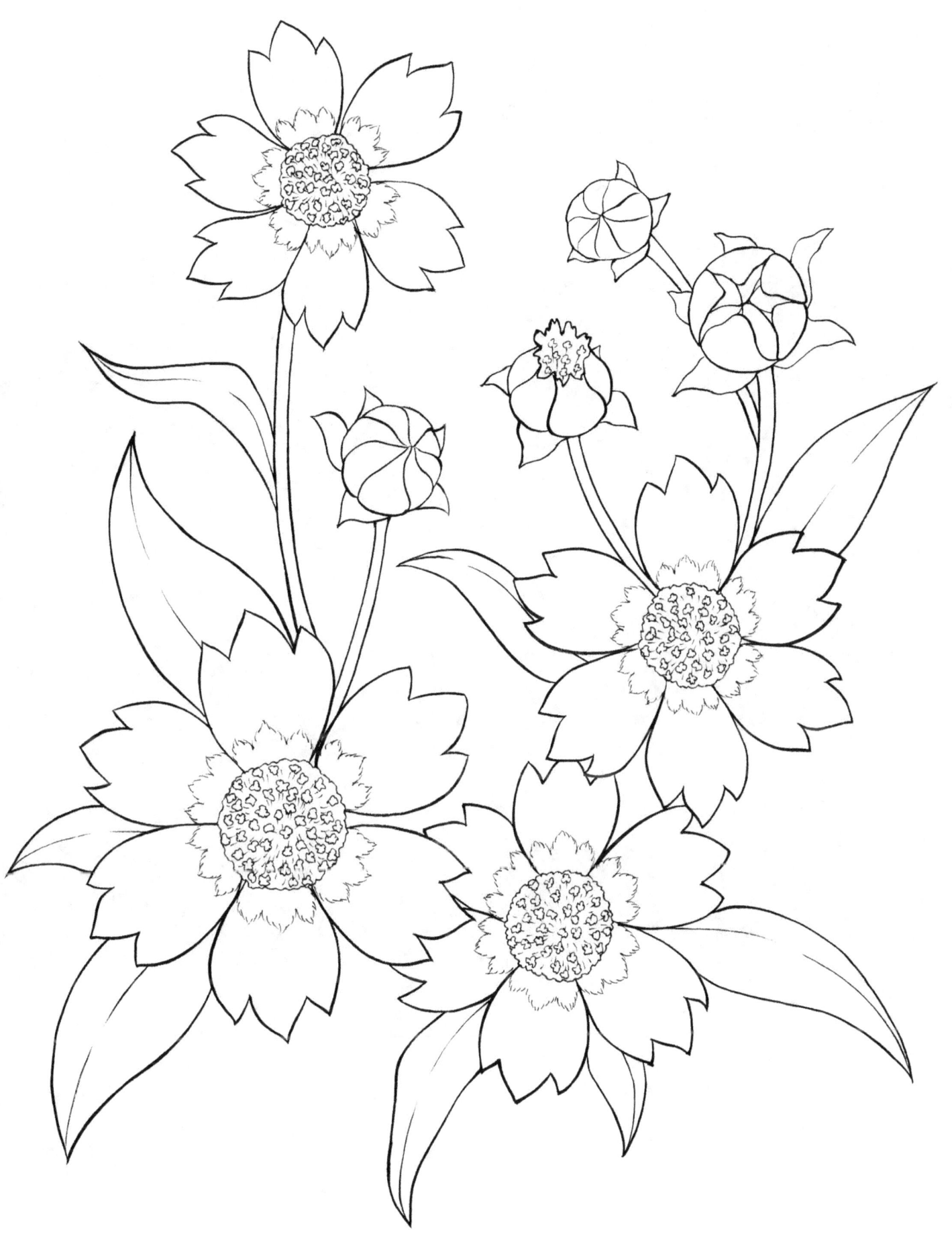